100 years with Carlisle City Fire Brigade

from the days of the horses until 1975

by J.P. Templeton

European Library   ZALTBOMMEL/THE NETHERLANDS

Acknowledgements:
The compiler ex-fireman J.P. Templeton would like to thank all who have assisted in the production of this book, with a special thanks to Elizabeth.
The book is also in memory of all comrades who have served on Carlisle City Fire Brigade past and present.

**Armorial Bearings
of the
City of Carlisle**

ARMS – Gold a cross formy between four roses gules with another on the cross gold.
SUPPORTERS – Two Wyverns gules their wings sterwn with golden roses.
The shield ensigned with a mural crown of cold–

GB ISBN 90 288 6120 3 / CIP

© 1995 European Library – Zaltbommel/The Netherlands

No part of this book may be reproduced in any form, by print, photoprint, microfilm or any other means, without written permission from the publisher.

The Uncharted Years

Although the city of Carlisle records that the city was virtually destroyed by fire on three occasions – 1251, again in 1292 and finally in 1390 – there is very little evidence of any firefighting parties until the late 18th century, when insurance companies began to take an interest in the protection from fire of those properties which were insured by them.

Initially, fire engines and squirts or syringes were employed by the Romans, and as Carlisle was an important civil settlement for the two hundred years plus of its occupation, there may have been appliances in the city 1,700 years ago. To date no traces have been found, but it is believed that the Roman engine consisted of two cylinders and pistons connected to a reciprocating beam, which raised and lowered the piston alternatively. The jet of water tended to be weak, as the pressure ceased at each stroke.

With the fall of Rome in 449 A.D. England lost many of the benefits of civilisation, and during the Dark Ages, we know nothing of how the citizen was protected from the 'scourge of fire'. However, among the benefits that William the Conqueror introduced was the General Curfew, – a bell was rang in the towns, villages and hamlets in the evenings, as a signal for all the citizens to put out their fires, for in those days houses had no fireplaces or chimneys. Carlisle's first Charter probably dates from 1158, when Henry II, who had retaken the city from the Scots, gave the city its first constitution and it is probable that the eight Trade Guilds, which until the passing of the Great Reform Act of 1832 bore their share in governing the city, had a system of fire fighting. This assumption is based on continuous border warring, and on the high proportion of old wooden buildings within the city walls.

No doubt the city possessed hand-squirt pumps during the middle ages. These were in general use throughout England until the close of the seventeenth century, and in the corporation records of 1561 ('The Dormant Book') the ordnance states that 'all men shall be in readiness immediately to come to a fray or soden fyer'. Failure to comply brought punishment and in the case of a Freeman, the offender was discharged of his 'frelege'. Evidently the threat of fire was treated with all seriousness. Fortunately, records exist which tell us of two fires toward the close of the eighteenth century.

1793: on an evening in January, a fire broke out at a house in Caldewgate completely demolishing it, but the exertions of the neighbours extinguished it before it could spread elsewhere. The city manual fire 'engine' was so much out of order as to be of little use.

1797: another outbreak of fire in English Street was quelled by a small fire engine belonging to the Castle. The extent of damage resulting from the inadequacy of this one small engine prompted a subscription to be made for the purchase of two new engines for the city.

The two engines bought (and described by Jollie), were a 3½" cylinder machine requiring six men to operate and a 5" cylinder requiring twelve men. In the event of fire, the keys were obtainable from Mr. Thomas Thompson of Scotch Street and Mr. Goodfellow of St. Cuthbert's Lane.

The earliest statutory reference to local fire engines that has been recorded is in the Carlisle Improvement Act of 1804 – one clause of which empowered the Commissioner to purchase 'fire engines, pipes, buckets and other items belonging thereto and pay and defray all cost, charges and expenses attending the same'. This would appear to be the beginning of the apparent duality of control over the city fire fighting appliances, as along with the Mayor and Alderman, others joined them as Commissioners to administer the Act. The city, however, did not assume the sole responsibility of fire prevention and control until the Carlisle New Volunteer Fire Brigade was absorbed seventy years later.

Although fire fighting appliances were purchased according to the position of the 1804 Act, Jollie in his 'Guide and Directory to Cumberland', published in 1811, stated: 'We think it necessary to mention that two fire engines are kept behind the East Walls. Unfortunately there are no firemen to man them in the event of fire.' This 'fire engine station' served until September 1837.

The next Act of Importance was the Carlisle Improvement Act of 1827. This was prompted by the Mayor and Alderman and the Dean and Chapter of the Cathedral. As in the earlier Act, the Commissioners were empowered to provide fire engines and also to contract for the care of such apparatus owned by the city and order the same to be used in 'case of fire or for the purpose of watering the streets'.

The next positive step was the forming of a group of 'volunteers' to man the appliances and fight any fire within the city. This too came about in 1827 and it is recorded of the volunteers that some were not 'ideal in their conduct'.

In the same year, the Mayor issued an order that in the case of a fire the practice of ringing the Town Hall bell should cease, because it succeeded in gathering 'improper persons' at the scene of the fire and brawling was not uncommon (subsequently supported by the Police Act).

In the event of a fire in the countryside during this period, news of the outbreak was sent to Carlisle by dispatch of a telegram or by horse rider and in one case of a rural outbreak, the local firemen refused to turn out until they were given their beer money. This money was a token payment to 'the rabbel' volunteers for proffering their services.

Set against this precarious background the task of defending Carlisle, small though it was, from outbreaks of fire was for the most parts in the hands of a number of the most important insurance companies of that time ('the professionals!'): The Sun,

Norwich Union, The Lion, Phoenix, The Royal, The Globe, The Atlas, and Bristol. Indeed, these insurance companies actively stimulated public interest in fire prevention and 'very handsomely' subscribed to the subsequent Fire Engine Fund. Although they did not keep major appliances in a small city such as Carlisle, in the larger towns such as Liverpool and Birmingham each company had its own fire engine and, of course, would only deal with a fire belonging to them. That is to say, their sign, probably of tin in the 1830's, had to be on the wall of the named building. Today there is only one of these signs in existence within Carlisle. The most notable being in Fisher Street affixed to the premises of 'Connons Shop'.

Also about this period, the Police Fire Brigade under the command of a head constable with a force of four sergeants and twenty-five constables came into being. This force, dependent upon the corporation for its appliances, worked with the 'volunteers', although rivalry was not always confined to the background, and exchanges between hoses and flared tempers was not unknown.

This system of control remained unaltered and it was not until the reformed council came into being in 1836, as a consequence of the Municipal Corporation Act of 1835, that the Council as a body gave more attention to the service.

'The rabbel'

Modern Carlisle can be said to date from the middle of the eighteenth century, between the 1745 Jacobite Rising and 1800. In this period a considerable amount of new premises and factories were established and controlled mainly by men who were not eligible to become Freemen of the city and therefore had no share in municipal affairs – 'Incomers'. These manufacturers sponsored an Act of Parliament in 1810, which stimulated the passage of the Municipal Corporation Act of 1835, thus removing the Freeman's monopoly in civic affairs, and subsequently, a number of manufacturers were elected to the City Council.

The Act of 1835 made a clean sweep of the Council ('new brooms sweep clean'). The newly-elected City Council were fire conscious and regarded the old machines bought in the provision of the 1804-1810 Acts as being obsolete. These engines were scheduled for sale, only to be replaced by 'two… more powerful and better constructed (fire engines)'… Carlisle Patriot, March 1836.

On 16th April it transpired: 'We are glad to learn that in accordance with a hint which we threw out a few weeks ago, some spirited gentlemen (tradesmen) have commenced a subscription for the purpose of purchasing an efficient fire engine, with buckets, hose and up to date fittings, to be used in the calamity of fire'. The management of which was to be placed in 'competent hands'. Amongst the list of subscribers we find the fire insurance companies and most of the opulent manufacturers of the city.

Indeed, this list was published in the local papers in order to 'induce some who have not yet come forward to subscribe their sum'.

28th April 1842
Report of the Fire Engine Committee
That they have received the undermentioned sums from the different Fire assurance offices manned to reward the officers and others who were active in assisting to extinguish the late **Fire at the Angel Inn** in English Street on the morning of Saturday the 12th March last which they have divided as per annexed list.

	£	s	d
Mr. R. Backhouse – Agent to the Atlas Assurance Fire Office	3	0	0
Mr. W. Martindale – Agent to Phoenix -do-	1	10	0
Mr. Wm. Stordy – Agent to the York & London -do-	1	10	0
	£6	0	0

John Graham Supt.	10s	6d	William Storrow		3s	0d
Thomas Hetherington	9s	1½d	William Johnston		3s	0d
Henry Dyer	5s	0d	Samuel Watson		5s	0d
John Kent	3s	0d	Edward Wallace		3s	0d
Joseph Haugh	3s	0d	Fergus Murray		9s	0d
John Barnfather	3s	0d	Thomas Milburn		3s	0d
John Johnston	3s	0d	Moffat		5s	0d
Robert Robinson	5s	0d	Joseph Cook		3s	0d
George Baty	3s	0d	Thomas Sewell		3s	0d
Matthew Corcoran	3s	0d	William Todd		3s	0d
John Robertson	5s	0d	John Murray		3s	0d
Richard Barnfather	3s	0d			£2.3s.	0d
Thomas Coil	3s	0d			£3.1s.	7½d
Thomas Ruddick	3s	0d	Pair Trousers for			
	£3.1s.	7½d	Thos. Hetherington	15s	4½d	
				£6.0s.0d		

Adjourned to Thurday the 5th May next at 7 o'clock in the evening.

Joseph Railton

Local momentum for securing a good organised fire fighting force increased when on 22nd April 1836...

Carlisle Patriot, April 22nd 1836

Mr. Richardson who gave special notice of motion to the effect that £50 should be presented from the funds of the corporation towards a fund for raising fire engines, rescinded that notice, and stated that as the subscription had already proved sufficient for one engine, he would move that the Watch Committee be instructed to pay over £100 towards another fire engine which the town required very much. Note Alderman Hunton strongly censured the mode of going about the town begging for such a necessary purpose.

The subscription was not voluntary, Mr. Brown, the banker, and his conjuctors on the Committee, had taken from the Town funds nearly £400. **Alderman Hunton**: I am sorry to say that everything named on the score of practical improvement in the town has been received very coldly and in fact put down.

Mr. Sheffield: I cannot see any harm in this subscription, it is voluntary.

Alderman Hunton explained and the motion that £100 be paid to the Watch Committee, towards the Fire Engine Fund, if they think proper, then proposed by Mr. W. Richardson, seconded by Mr. Weir, and carried.

Such a 'magnificent sum' was raised by public subscription, that a new fire station was bought and stationed at West Walls, adjacent to the Police Office. This building carries the initials of George G. Mounsey, the first 'Reform Mayor'. The new engines called the 'Alert' and the 'City', built by Broadwood of London, were mounted on springs with spoked wheels and 'had each a dragpole enabling the use of horses'. So inarticulate were those machines that each required eighteen men to operate it.

The new engine house was a modernised wardhouse (being once a hospital), designed to accommodate the engines and provisioned rooms for a person to reside in. For the first time a position was created to command the post of 'caretaker of the fire engines' under the watchful eye of a uniformed superintendent and a night watchman. These men, together with city volunteers, were issued with instructions for the 'management of the fire engines', and in January 1837 the watchmen were given permission by the Watch Committee to break down doors in order that 'such fires may be extinguished as soon as possible'. It is also known from Watch Committee records that the machines were kept in a relatively high state of efficiency through Council funding, although they proved to be a mere token gesture at any conflagration.

Important fires of this era included: 1838: 'The Carlisle Patriot' rendered the first local newspaper report of a fire, at Stoddart & Rennies Warehouse, Willowholme, Carlisle. 1839: Newlaithes Hall on fire. 1840: A Caldewgate fire destroyed 3, Rigg Street, tenements. Subscriptions were asked for the homeless. This was met by the Sun Insurance Company. 1841: Whitrigg – disastrous fire at farm house; the same year Mr. Routledge's cotton mill was completely destroyed by fire. And on 7th January at 5.30 a.m. a fire broke out at Mrs. Brockbank's timber yard, near the canal basin, which was extinguished in two hours. In recognition of the service rendered, £5.0s.0d was donated both by the York and London Insurance Companies and Mrs. Brockbank (see Watch Committee Report of 28th January 1841). 1843: Netherby Hall on fire. 1845: Eleven serious fires include the Naworth Castle fire – fifty workmen engaged repairing damage; fire at Print Mill Works of Halliley & Co. Wigton – 'serious damage'. 1853: the Knells on fire. A fire in a Workington Ship Yard, help asked for by telegram. 1859: Shaws Hotel, Gilsland, destroyed by fire. And Dixons Factory on fire and checked before great damage done. 1864: Carlisle Engine Sheds destroyed by fire. 1866: Carlisle Flour Mill gutted. And the same year Beetle Works, Shaddongate, gutted by fire.

Hence, from a body partially evolved from public subscription and Council sponsorship, existed the nucleus for something greater. With the Victorian world becoming fire conscious and the spirit of inventiveness sweeping Europe, new measures for extinguishing outbreaks of fire were being patented in an ever increasing rate.
The Carlisle early volunteers had opened the gate for a more coherent and greater organised body of 'New Volunteers'. This revolution came about in 1866.

Captain J.A. Wheatley and the New Volunteer Fire Brigade

From 29th August 1866, Carlisle was to have an efficient Volunteer Fire Brigade, under the command of their Captain, Mr. J. A. Wheatley. On this summer evening, a public meeting was held in the Town Hall under the presidency of J. Huthart, Esq., Mayor, at which it was unanimously resolved to organise a Volunteer Fire Brigade for Carlisle.

The Castle Mill fire, three weeks before the meeting, gave the Reverend J.E. Hargreaves the idea for a volunteer fire fighting force: he was not the first who saw the necessity of a fire brigade in Carlisle, but he was the first who brought the matter practically before the citizens. Thus the Reverend Hargreaves, together with Wheatley, gave birth to the term Carlisle Volunteer Fire Brigade (C.V.F.B.) at the gathering.

The meetings attention was drawn to the frequency of outbreaks of fire (1860: 2 fires; 1861: 3 fires; 1862: 4 fires, 1863: 6 fires; 1864: 4 fires; 1865: 3 fires; 1866: 5 fires) and the Reverend pointed out the 'evils' arising from leaving the fire engines in the hands of the Police, especially where the force was so small as in Carlisle. If a fire broke out requiring the attendance of all the force, a premium was offered to thieves. In addition, Police firemen sometimes could not work the outdated machines 'satisfactorily' and generally too, the volunteers were 'not of the best class' and would not work without 'beer money'.

This factor gave rise to a 5/– entrance fee for membership to the brigade, thus both preventing 'undesirables' participating, and raising capital for the venture.

During the first year, August 1866-1867, the brigade met twenty-eight times for drill and simulation exercises, being an average of twice a month, and the number of members averaged thirty. The first year saw the brigade called out four times on alarm of fire, and on every occasion, the members had been found ready for active duty. It is of interest to note that to increase efficiency, boys were used to call the alarm and citizens employed to man the pumps at fires.

The new Fire Brigade Committee felt a great want of some system for speedily alarming and calling the men together. Lists of members and their addresses were prepared for the use of the Police, the idea being that the Police would alert the volunteers. However, this list was never used, because the Police resented their efficient rivals and, against Watch Committee orders, failed to comply with the instruction. As a consequence, permission was granted by the Dean and Chapter for the use of the Cathedral bells as an alarm in the case of fire, 'a boon which cannot be too highly appreciated'. The length of the bell pealing donated the seriousness of the fire. Later a 55 lb brass bell was locally constructed and given to the volunteers, the 'proud symbol' being mounted aloft the engine house. Even the military authorities in the castle joined in, and granted permission to the brigade to erect a gymnasium in the outer bailey drying yard.

The progress achieved was summarised in a letter by the Reverend Hargreaves:

The brigade have hitherto availed themselves of the permission granted by the Watch Committee, and have used one of the city engines for practice. The want of a third engine, however, having been long felt, your committee are glad to say that want is now supplied through the kindness and indefatigable exertions of Mr. T. L. BONNILL, who in a short time procured sufficient funds to purchase a new engine with complete equipment, and a fire-escape, for the benefit of the city. It is a source of great pride and gratification to the brigade that the Corporation have decided upon entrusting them with the charge and use of the new engine, and have caused to be erected an engine-house for its reception in the Shambles, the alterations in connections with which have been carried out under the able direction of Mr. MORLEY, the city surveyor.

Your committee are happy to say that the engine has been this day lodged in its new house, and they have taken upon themselves the responsibility of keeping and using it for the benefit of their fellow-citizens.

By the kind permission of the military authorities, the use of the drying ground in the Castle has been granted, where a gymnasium has been erected for the use of the brigade; and your committee hope that the members, to render themselves more efficient, will freely avail themselves of its advantages.

Your committe are also happy to present to your notice the financial statement, which shows a balance in hand of £22. 18s 11d., and they are now prepared to receive the names of gentlemen who are desirous of joining the brigade, and hope soon to bring up their number to the full complement recommended by the public meeting and in order to accomplish this they ask your approval of this report and your continued support and sympathy.

Your committee would also notice the assistance rendered to the movement by the Press, which has been at all times ready to advocate its claims; and they congratulate the citizens on their hitherto comparative exemption from severe conflagrations, but they trust that should the emergency arise, the organisation of the brigade and the courage and determination of its members will be found of the greatest service in coping with the destructive element.

Signed on behalf of the Committee,
JAMES E. HARGREAVES, Hon. Sec.

Looking to the immediate future a need was acknowledged for the hand engines to be distributed to firemen residing in suitable districts of the town, thus when an alarm of fire was given, they were immediately on the spot to subdue the fire or to retard its progress until the arrival of the larger engines. To raise sufficient funds to cover these requirements the Watch Committee employed an agent, to collect from 'those who hope to receive the benefit of their (the C.V.F.B.'s) service'.

To maintain a highly efficient brigade, both the City Surveyor and Sub-Committee annually inspected the apparatus and appliances, making independent reports about all aspects of the service. As a consequence of such reports and the growing prosperity of the city, by 1869 a powerful new engine, a Shand, Mason & Co., horse-drawn vehicle was bought, fitted with hose, fire-escape ladders and other appliances. Similarly, L'Extincteurs, provided by the Corporation were stationed in

the engine house and Town Hall, and six manual engines, bought with public subscriptions, were allocated to members of the brigade in suitable parts of the city.
The shortage of fires was such, that the engineers of the brigade had time to modify and experiment with their appliances, hence a powerful lever drag was designed and mounted on the large engine as a stabilising safeguard, and clamps added to the leather hoses to stop leakage. Concurrently a fire at the County Mews illuminated the need for the modification of the water plugs and 'proper indicators' of the city. (These were water sources into which the hose pumps were fastened.)
At this time however, despite the eagerness of the brigade, the time of the outbreak of fire depended if your premises were to be saved or not, thus on a Saturday evening when the members were absorbed in their 'several avocations' the public was statistically at greater risk to fire damage.

The most serious fire since the formation of the brigade came on 10th January 1871 at Slaters Cotton Mill, in which an employee lost his life and the conflagration consequently deprived 170 people of a means of livelihood. The building, being seventy years old, was built of combustible materials, saturated with oil and without partitions to isolate the outbreak 'from the free passage of air.' The Police force, now under the charge of a sergeant, while the engine was manned by constables, joined with the 32 volunteers and together prevented the spread of the fire to surrounding buildings.

The Brigade in Action

NEWSPAPER REPORTS 1867-1868

Fire in Carlisle

Last night there was to be witnessed a very exciting scene in Scotch Street. About half past eight dense streams of smoke were observed to come through the crevices of the shutters on the shop of Mr. France Elliot, hatter; and, with surprising rapidity, an immense and noisy crowd assembled round the place, to whom the few minutes of necessary delay in getting up the engines seemed terribly tantalising, for the smoke increased in density, and only the little milliner's shop of Miss Armstrong stood between the seat of fire and Mr. Harrison's gunsmith's premises. Mr. Councillor Bewley and others prevented the taking down of the shutters until the machine arrived, lest the influx of air might give the flames new life; but the moment the rattle of one engine was heard, down at once came the shutters, and out rushed volumes of black smoke which enveloped the entire front; and immediately the police with their engine and the Volunteer Fire Brigade with theirs dashed up almost simultaneously. However, it was soon found that there was no occasion for the help they had so very speedily brought. The fire was burning at the back part of the premises, part of the doorway in the lane, and the goods near it inside, being partly consumed; but a few well-directed buckets of water put an end to all apprehension. The damage done is considerable. We are informed that a short while before a juvenile fired some gunpowder beside the door; and the likely theory is that the fire originated therefrom. Very great credit indeed is due to the police and to the Fire Brigade for turning out so promptly. Captain Wheatley and twelve of his men drew up in a very few minutes, and their vigour was acknowledged by the crowd with cheers.

Fire in Carlisle

About five o'clock yesterday (Thursday) morning one of the policemen on duty in Botchergate discovered that a fire had broken out on the premises occupied by Mr. Swan, grocer, and picture frame maker, London Road. He immediately gave the alarm to the other policemen on duty, who at once proceeded to the police office, got out a fire engine, and under the superintendence of Sergeants Cowin and Anderson were soon on the spot. A plentiful supply of water was obtained from an hydrant which was close at hand; and they had nearly got the flames subdued, when about fourteen members of the Carlisle Volunteer Fire Brigade, to whom the alarm had been given at about 5.15 a.m., arrived with another engine under the command of Captain Wheatley. Finding that their engine was not required, they relieved the policemen at the pumps, and by six o'clock the fire was extinguished. The fire is supposed to have broken out in an upstair room used as a kitchen, which before being discovered had extended to a bedroom adjoining, in which a man was sleeping, but who, together with Mrs. Swan, who was sleeping in another room, had fortunately been warned of the dangerous position in which they were placed, by a person throwing a brick through the window. The whole of the ceiling of the kitchen is destroyed, and the stock amongst which was a number of pictures valued at about £100 is also much damaged, the pictures being rendered worthless. The ceiling of the bedroom is also damaged. The property and stock are insured. The origin of the fire is unknown, but it is conjectured that it has arisen from the joists of the ceiling of the kitchen, which are built into the flue of the chimney, having taken fire.

Fire in Scotch Street

A little before one o'clock this (Friday) morning a fire which but for the timely discovery might have been disastrous in its results, broke out in the shop of Mr. R. Shaw, grocer and provision dealer, Scotch Street, in this city. P.C. Rutherford, who was on duty in Scotch Street, while a short distance from the shop, saw a volume of smoke issuing from a portion of the building. At first he thought it proceeded from the Examiner office, whose printing establishment is behind the premises already named, but on going towards the place found that the smoke was issuing from the grocer's shop. He was to summon the police and Mr. Bent, but in the meantime several members of the Volunteer Fire Brigade living in the neighbourhood of the fire, speedily got out the engine which was close at hand in the Shambles. It was found, however, that the fire was within manageable proportions, and a number of volunteers offering their services and a good supply of water being obtained from Mr. James' house, the fire was extinguished without the use of the brigade engine or the police engine, which shortly afterwards arrived. It is supposed that the fire broke out in a room immediately behind Mr. Shaw's shop, owing to some clothes and other articles of a combustible nature, which were before the fire, having ignited and extended to the floor above. Great alarm was caused least the fire should spread to Mr. James' tallow chandlery which is close by.

Fire in Botchergate

On Sunday morning, at 3.30, a fire broke out in a bakehouse belonging to Mr. Robinson, East Street, Botchergate. The alarm was given simultaneously by Police sergeant Anderson and by Mr. Mathews, a member of the Fire Brigade, who resides in the adjoining house. The result was that the two engines arrived within a few minutes of each other, and the police fixed their hose to the hydrant in East Street, whilst the Fire Brigade took the back of the premises in a lane leading off Portland Place. It was found in a few minutes that the fire was only assailable from the latter point, and it soon succumbed to the well-directed efforts of the volunteers. The fire was discovered to be in a quantity of peats stored near the oven, and its rapid suppression affords another instance of the value of an organisation which prevents a serious loss to property by the rapidity with which the fire is suppressed immediately on its discovery. The damage done is trifling, and will be covered by insurance in the London, Liverpool, and Globe Fire Office.

Second Edition Journal Office, 5.30 a.m.

Fire at Messrs. Carr's works this morning

This morning about five o'clock a fire was discovered upon the premises of Messrs. Carr and Company's biscuit factory, Caldewgate; but fortunately it was extinguished before much damage was done. As a carter was going to the stable to attend to his horses, he observed smoke issuing from the packing room. He at once gave the alarm, and the workmen from Messrs. Carr and Company's breadworks on the opposite side of the road, who were already at their work, hurried to the spot, and by the means of hose kept upon the premises, and by the application of 'extincteurs', the fire was soon put out. In the meantime the factory bell had been rung, the 'buzzer' at the Gas Works had been sounded. The fire-engines were got out and taken towards the scene of alarm with great speed but fortunately their services were not required, as all danger had passed and the fire had been completely extinguished before the engines reached the works. The damage done is very trifling.

11th December 1868

Alarm of Fire – Shortly before ten o'clock on Tuesday morning, considerable commotion was occasioned in different parts of this city by an alarm of fire. The alarming intelligence was conveyed to the Carlisle Volunteer Fire Brigade that a conflagration was devastating the premises of the Co-operative Society's stores in Botchergate; and accordingly the fire bell was rung, and the firemen, responsive to its summons, quickly congregated at their engine-house in the butchers' shambles. A scout was despatched, while the engine was getting ready, to ascertain what proportions the fire had assumed; but upon his arrival in Botchergate no signs of a fire could be seen, and he was informed that it was at the Co-operative Society's stores in Caldewgate where the services of the brigade were required. Accordingly the engine and its attendant firemen dashed off into that locality; but there, too, everything was still – neither smoke nor flame was visible, – and the whole affair turned out to be a hoax.

NEWSPAPER REPORTS – 1872

Alarming fire at Holme Head Cotton Mill

On Tuesday morning last, a fire occurred in one of the spinning rooms at Messrs. Fergusons' factory, and but for the admirable provision which is made on the premises for such an emergency, we would have had to-day to record a great calamity. About half-past five, before the workers had come, the watchman was lighting the gas, when a spark dropped from his lamp upon some cotton bloom which had settled on the machinery below, and which 'fired like gunpowder'. In a moment the flames were beyond the control of the watchman and his assistant, and they therefore raised the alarm outside with all speed. The call was promptly responded to, for very soon there were numbers of hearty workers who rendered good service with buckets. One of the earliest to arrive was Sergeant-Major Rodney, who is sub-engineer of the fire-brigade, and who went right into the room with the hand-engine that is kept at his house. The factory is fitted up with shafts connected with the boiler house, by means of which volumes of steam can be discharged into any room; and in this way the atmosphere were rendered so humid that the flames could scarcely make headway. The alarm had been carried to the Police Office, and as the men were just coming off their beats, they, under the direction of Sergeants Cowen, Stordy, and Phillips, were at the scene as speedily as they could drag their engine through the quagmire of Denton Street. A little later, the Fire Brigade, who had been delayed for horses, reached Holme Head, in charge of Mr. J.S. Bell, the engineer, and Mr. Davidson, the foreman, Captain Wheatley joining them shortly afterwards. The spectacle was a very exciting one for some time, the disaster which seemed to impend being one of serious importance to the people of the district; but the firemen skilfully and successfully repulsed the efforts of the flames to invade fresh ground; the glass screen which divides the room prevented a current of air; and everything being favourable, the fire was got under control shortly after seven. The damage is not so extensive as was at first reported; and it is covered by insurance.

Incendiary fire in Carlisle

On Tuesday evening last a fire broke out in a building near Carlisle Gas Works, at present unoccupied, but lately used as a saw-mill by Mr. John Brockbank. It was discovered by the woman in charge of the building, who was going round the yard about five o'clock, and saw smoke issuing from the old saw-mill. He at once gave an alarm, and Mr. Hepworth, manager of the Gas Works, promptly sent over an extincteur in charge of a man named Huthart, who upon entering the building discovered a considerable body of fire just bursting into flame and issuing from under the sides of the flooring. The extincteur was played upon the fire with considerable effect, and by the time it was exhausted a hand engine belonging to the Volunteer Fire Brigade arrived, in charge of Shields, of Water Street. This had the effect of extinguishing the fire. The alarm, however, having been given by the buzzer, the police engine was quickly on the spot, in charge of Sergeant Cowen, and the hose was attached and the place received a thorough drenching to guard against any fresh outbreak of fire. The Volunteer Brigade engine was also on its way to the fire. The only damage done was to the flooring beyond which the fire was never allowed to make any progress. There were eighteen brigade men on the spot, many of them in uniform, and great activity was displayed by Mr. Hepworth, Mr. Lees, Huthart, and Thompson in their voluntary work. The origin of the fire was for some time in doubt, but it was generally considered that it was the result of incendiarism. Yesterday this doubt was cleared up by the police, who apprehended two boys on a charge of setting the place on fire. Their names are George Macmillan, nine years old, and William Macmillan, seven years old. From the statements of the boys it appears that a boy named Edmund Barton, ten years old, was in company with them at the time; and the police are on the look out for him, but have not yet apprehended him. The boys in custody say they obtained admission to the sawmill by creeping through a hole in the wall, and that when there the elder of the Macmillans, who had matches in his possession, piled some chips of sawdust and set fire to the heap.

Fire at the Carlisle Gas Works

Yesterday afternoon, a fire broke out at the Gas Works, in this city, which might have been fraught with the most disastrous consequences. The scene of the conflagration was the retort-house, a large fire-proof building, situated at the side of the Gas Works nearest Messrs. Nelson's marble works. At about twenty-five minutes before four o'clock, one of the pipes used for the purpose of conveying tar, cracked, and the tar escaping came in connection with one of the retorts near the centre of the building, and blazed up most furiously. Indeed, in less time than it takes to write it, the centre of the large building was one sheet of flame up to the roof. From the openings in the roof the smoke issued in thick clouds, and soon cast a gloom over the neighbourhood, which told the inhabitants that everything was not right at the Gas Works. Consequently, in a short time, a very large crowd had congregated outside the gates. The city fire engine, under the command of Mr. Bent, was soon on the spot, and almost as soon in working order. A plentiful supply of water was at hand, and the hose was directed to where the blaze was raging fiercest. At first the extending flames seemed to lap up the shower of water and then rage on more furiously. By a few minutes past four the members of the Volunteer Fire Brigade, many of them in uniform, under the command of Captain Wheatley, were on the scene with their new engine, which they placed at the opposite end of the retort-house to the police engine. The hose was then carried to a side door immediately opposite the flaming fire, from which point they played on the retort very vigorously and with good effect. Meanwhile the police engine had been worked with a will, and had done capital service. It was only when there was any relaxation of efforts that the fire gained a momentary victory, but this was soon overcome by the strong stream of water, and, after some continuous working at the pumps, it was apparent that the destructive element was being routed. Within an hour and five minutes of the outbreak all signs of danger had been dispelled, and though dense volumes of smoke continued to issue from the openings in the roof, no fire of any amount was to be seen inside. During the time that the fire was raging, and for some time after, the air of the neighbourhood had a strong smell of burning tar, and the smoke lowered over the streets. The members of the Volunteer Fire Brigade worked remarkably well and were of great service, the orders of Captain Wheatley being carried out with great punctuality by the men. The police, from being first on the scene, had an advantage over the brigade, and had done a great deal to check the flames before the volunteers got fairly to work. Both, however, may work together with advantage to the town, and none but the most prejudiced will say that the brigade did not do good service on Friday. An immense crowd of people assembled in front of the gasworks, on the Bush Brow, and on Nelson Bridge during the fire, and on leaving the gasworks yard the Fire Brigade was loudly applauded. To the fact that the retort-house was built of fire-proof material may be attributed to the fire extending no further, for if the building had been built of inflammable stuff, it must inevitably have been burned to the ground, had the fire perhaps extended further, disastrous consequences would have been the result, as the gasometers are not far off. Fortunately the blaze was attacked in time. The damage done was not very much.

In 1872 several additional hand engines were purchased and located throughout the city, thus there was no district in Carlisle without one of these safeguards, and housewives were encouraged to make themselves familiar with the whereabouts of their nearest station, indicated by a number plate affixed to the residence of the fireman in charge.

Hand-engine stations 1872
LIST OF MEMBERS
To whom the Alarm may be given in case of fire, and the Persons giving the Alarm will be Rewarded.

J. A. Wheatley (CAPTAIN)
  Day Address — English Street
  Night Address — 2 Devonshire Terrace, Stanwix
W. Buckle, 38 Etterby Street, Stanwix
George Bell, Photographer, English Street
S. T. Barnes, 84 English Street (MINUTE SERGEANT)

S. Wright, Carlisle Square
* W. Davidson, 15 Globe Lane (FOREMAN)
Daniel Wilson, Globe Lane
E. W. Sibson, 9 Paternoster Row
G. Bell, Castle Street
J. Hallaway, 54 Castle Street
William Sanderson, Drovers' Lane
J. Denard, 2 Lowther Street
R. Westray, 13 Lowther Street
J. Bell, 31 Lowther Street
W. B. Nanson, Victoria Place
* J. Lees, 43 Chiswick Street (SERGEANT)
J. C. Mason, 45 Chiswick Street
* W. H. Wright, 4 Surtee's Lane, Botchergate
T. Matthews, 7 East Street, Botchergate
William Noble, Brisco's Place, Princes' Street
John Tinning, 108 Collier's Lane
* T. H. Simpson, Tait Street (SERGEANT)
* J. L. Shields, Water Street
J. Cunningham, Water Street
E. Cunningham, Water Street
W. H. Graham, Long Island Works
* J. Rodney, Norfolk Street (SUB-ENGINEER)
J. Johnston, Charlotte Street
T. Little, Slack's Court, Milburn Street
* John Smith, 27 Shaddongate
J. Shaw, 13 Devonshire Walk
* These were hand-engine stations.

Other important changes came with a new method of alarming the members of an outbreak of fire, by the acquisition of a steam buzzer which was installed at the Corporation Gas Works (one blast fire in town, two blasts fire in country); the brass fire bell being moved to the Police Station for a more 'efficient' means of communication between the two bodies. The public, too, were again brought into the campaign for raising a speedy alarm by advertisements, the gist of which read: 'Persons giving an alarm of fire will be rewarded.' Speed thus was the very essence of fire fighting and in 1873, the brigade made an agreement with the Citadel Station to provide a 'waggon' to convey their engine to fires in the country.

By 1875, new rooms were found at Victoria Buildings, Lowther Street, this provided a store room, library and reading room, committee room and headquarters for the brigade. Property which was scattered throughout the town could now be congregated in the one spot. Captain Williams, 'the gallant and experienced' Chief of Edinburgh Fire Brigade, inspected the new headquarters, suggesting possible improvements and complimenting the brigade on their drill and efficiency.

The following year saw the establishment of a new fire engine fund with the object of providing a special engine to be stationed in the Caldewgate/Delton Holme district, at a cost of £140.0.0.

To stimulate public awareness, four lists of the names of subscribers were published every other week in the local press. Money featured very prominently in the affairs of the brigade in 1877, because, as a result of a major refit – i.e. uniforms, equipment, badges, helmets, belts and hatchets, sundries for carriage, new extincteurs, jumping sheets and laterns – the brigade for the first time faced a deficit in its accounts. The pretext behind this buying was prompted by two factors. Firstly, the major premise, being to accommodate a reception and visit by the Princess Louise, secondly, the ranks had swelled to 48 firemen.

During the same year as Princess Louise's visit, we find the two biggest engines position thus: –
No. 1 Engine: Engineers J. Bell and J. Rodney; Sub Engineer T. Simpson; Sergeant W. Burke and Minute Sergeant J. Mason.
The Volunteer: at Butcher Market, Scotch Street.
No. 2 Engine: Engineers B. Simpson and J. Shield; Sub Engineer J. Armstrong; Sergeant Wm. Maxwell and Minute Sergeant R. Little.
The Alert: at Beetling Works, Shaddongate (temporary site).

As disclosed, the worst time for dealing with a fire was late on a Saterday evening. This occasioned on 11th September 1880 at a pawnbrokers in Fisher Street.

An excited and unruly mob were on the spot before the engines arrived and being pressed into the narrow street, the efforts of the firemen and Police and by-standers willing to give real help, were greatly impeded though aided by a military force from the Castle. (At this point it should be remembered that while the volunteers made progress so did the Police force, who had always been a forefront of most of the City's fires.) A lot of valuable property was stolen and destroyed under the pretext of being saved from the fire, brawling broke out and convictions were made by the Police. It was also probable that some of the hoses were intentionally cut. This led to a liaison with the Police force, which enabled the firemen to fight the 'scourge' and the Police to concentrate their attention on ordinary duties of the Police force. In addition a system of drill by signal was created, which could be executed in perfect silence.

By 1881 the headquarters still lay at Lowther Street whilst the problem of finding a permanent site for the 'Alert', which lodged at the premises of Messrs. Hewson & Co., Shaddongate, still remained. This, however, was secondary to the bonus of acquiring two new engines.

The position was now:
The 'City' Engine: Adams, John (Sub-Engineer), Sowerby's Court, Duke Street; Bell, George (Engineer), 3 Carrick's Court, Water Street; Bell, Richard (Sergeant), 7 Crosby Street; Cumberland, John, 21 William Street; Cowie, James, Johnston's Court, South John Street; Cowie, John, Gas Works; Heywood, Thomas, 50 Charlotte Street; Hadfield, James E., 16 Bridge Terrace, Holme Head; * Hepworth, J., Gas Works; Murphy, Owen, 1 South George Street; Matthews, Thomas (Sergeant), 10 Hawick Street; Shields, J.L., (Foreman), 67 Water Street; Shields, J.L., Jun., 55 South John Street; Wright, Samuel, 11 Carlisle Square.
The 'Alert' Engine: Armstrong, J. (Engineer), 5 Corries Court, Milbourne Street; Chesney, Alex., 9 Hope's Court, Port Road; Dawson, George, Belle Vue; Fleming, H., Thompson's Court, Church Street, Caldewgate; Hodgson, 9 Hawick Street; Little, Robert (Foreman), 109 Denton Street; Long, Robert, 36 Milbourne Street; Maxwell, William (Sub-Engineer), 64 Shaddongate; Moffat, J.G., 9 York Street; * Sanderson, Robert (Sergeant), Duke Street; Sanderson, Thomas, 7 Holme Court, Milbourne Street; Smith, John;
Warwick, John (Min.-Serg.), 17 Hope Street, Denton Holme.
The 'Waterwitch' Engine: Askew, Wm. John, 18 Myddleton Street; Anderson, Richard, 9 Solway Terrace; Bell, Edward (Sub-Engineer), 27 William Street; Doyle, John, Tyndale Court, Charlotte Street; Gardiner, Wm., 9 Barwise Court, English Street; Green, Joseph (Sergeant), 12 Peascod's Lane, English Street; Huthart, Wm. (Engineer), 2 Mill Street; Hawgood, R.H., 18 Finkle Street; Little, James (Foreman), 3 Bousfield's Lane, Scotch Street; Love, Samuel, St. Nicholas; McGill, Robert, 9 Sheffield Street; Stephenson, John, 5 Earl Street; * Wright, Thomas, Portland Place.
The 'Volunteer' Engine: * Buckle, Wilson (Sub-Engineer), 39 South Street; Bragg, John (Sergeant), 2 Delta Court, William Street; Bell, George, Friars Court, Devonshire Street; Brown, W.G., Barwise Court, English Street; Dent, Joseph, 14 Finkle Street; Fox, Joseph, Princess Street; Halliburton, William, 6 Close Street; McKie, John, Hartington Place; McKie, James, Hartington Place; Nanson, Wm. A., 3 Lonsdale Street; Rodney, Joseph (Foreman), Rifle Drill Hall; Routledge, Isaac B., Etterby Street, Stanwix; Sewell, William, Scotch Street; * Simpson, Thomas H., (Engineer), Aglionby Street; Weller, Isaac, 22 Duke Street.

In February 1881, a new policy in fire fighting was adopted. The Chief Constable and Watch Committee gave charge at fires of the whole of the engines and plant belonging to the Corporation, and consequently under the management of the Police, to the Volunteer Brigade. By supplementing the number of the brigade by twenty men, 'furnished with their outfit' and maintained by an annual vote, the authorities practically adopted and reorganised the brigade as the official organisation for the suppression of fire in Carlisle. The position was to be reversed twenty-three years later when the Police force took over the management of the brigade.

In 1885 the brigade moved the 'Alert' into its new station in Junction Street. These new premises at a cost of £466-5s-5d housed a permanent custodian engineer Sanderson. The building also served as a station for the newly-purchased hose-cart carrying 500 feet of the celebrated 'Rob Roy' canvas hose, with stand pipes and 'other necessary appliances', also a 'Tozer' hand engine and 'an extincteur(sic) of the newest construction'. The fire escape was also placed here as the Watch Committee considered it 'most likely' effective among the 'lofty factories' and other buildings in the densely-populated area. This building was placed in telegraphic communication with the Police Office, which in turn was in communication with the steam buzzer at the Gas Works – to ensure a speedy universal alert.

It was at this stage, that the brigade suffered the great loss of their founder, Captain J.A. Wheatley, who was forced to retire because of ill-health after eighteen years of service of the 'highest efficiency'.

The resignation letter:

Portland Square, Carlisle
Dec. 15th, 1884

Dear Mr. Mason, — The time has at length arrived when I feel that I can no longer defer placing in your hands, as Secretary, my resignation as Captain of the Volunteer Fire Brigade. In doing so, I beg to thank most heartily the officers and men of the Brigade for the confidence they have reposed in me during the long period of over eighteen years, and also for the kindness and courtesy I have always experienced from them in the performance of my duties. I sever my connection from the Brigade with extreme reluctance, and shall cherish the memories connected with it as among the pleasantest of my life. To you, personally, I am greatly indebted for the active support you have always given me in the discharge of your onerous official duties; and with kindest regards, and fervent hopes for the welfare and prosperity of the Brigade, I remain, dear Mr. Mason, yours very sincerely,

JAMES A. WHEATLEY

At the December 1884 meeting of the Fire Brigade Sub Committee, Lieutenant Bell was unanimously chosen to fill Captain Wheatley's post.

All horses at this time were hired from the local Mews, the cost being according to time and distances, for instance, in 1884, the cost for hiring horses were given as £9-1s-0d and cab hire at 3/6. This cost was a contributory factor when in February

1887, the Watch Committee considered 'the possibility of recovering a reasonable charge for the use of the fire engines belonging to the city outside the municipal boundary be obtained'. Duly a list of charges for the attendance of the fire brigade at surrounding parishes was sanctioned. (A 'retaining fee', subsequently supported by the Parish Fire Engine Act, 1898.)

For example, October 1905:

parish	annual retaining fee
Stanwix	£10-0-0
Wetheral	£ 7-0-0
Dalston	£ 6-6-0

Failure to pay the retaining fee meant that the use of the brigade 'would not be permitted' in the event of a fire.

In 1896, Spring Garden Lane, Lowther Street, was chosen for the erection of a new fire engine shed at a cost of £750, it included stables and 'all'. This was to be the brigade's headquarters for the next thirty-eight years.

The dawn of a new century (the Police era)

The beginning of a new century heralded a clean-out of the brigade archives. The manual fire engine positioned at Spring Garden Lane was moved to West Walls and used at country fires, and the obsolete manual fire engine at West Walls was sold. Similarly the fire escape at Spring Lane was removed to the Junction Street Station and the old fire escape sold.

Two years later, 1902, it was recommended the purchase of a horse-drawn steam fire engine at a cost of £425 and a fire escape at a cost of £92 from Messrs. Merryweather & Son, London SE. The brigade thus became mechanised and the new fire engine saw its action at the Tower fire of St. Cuthbert's Church 1904.

In keeping with the Liberal reforms which were sweeping the country during this period, on 7th September 1904, the Fire Brigade Committee sponsored a party of Brigade Officers to tour various towns of England 'to obtain information and report as to the best Fire Brigade system'. In December of the same year Captain J.J. Bell (the only remaining member of the brigade who joined at its foundation in 1866) enclosed a notice of resignation of the members of the C.V.F.B. as from '31st instance' to the Watch Committee.

The Town Clerk replied stating that the Chief Constable was to take over the fire station and all appliances as from the last day of the year, and that Captain Bell and his men should be in attendance at Spring Garden Lane at 4 p.m. that day to arrange the transfer and hand over all fire brigade property. The reorganisation cost the ratepayer 1/2d in the pound. Upon Captain Bell's retirement from the service, Captain J. Little under the patronage of the Chief Constable assumed command of the brigade. His term of office continued until 1908, when the Chief Constable, George Hill as 'director of the fire brigade' assumed overall control.

In March 1905, the Council delegated to the Watch Committee its powers under section 32 of the town Police Clause Act, 1847, as extended by the Police Act, 1893, to employ constables and permanent firemen. The supervisor of the Police firemen was Sergeant Wakeford (formerly of Oldham Fire Brigade), who was the City's first full-time fireman, being Station Officer and Training Officer. Fire duties were executed by constables who received 30/- for their Police work and an additional 5/- for their fire duties, being pensionable on appointment.

In keeping with the report, constable fireman Albert Dougdale (also of Oldham Fire Brigade) was appointed to live at Spring Garden Lane, and in February 1905 the National Telegraphic Co. set up communications between the Police Office and the houses of sixteen firemen constables and the public convenience in English Street. A public alarm was also erected at St. Nicholas at a cost of £4.0s.0d per annum.

The first year of operation saw 21 fires and introduced to Spring Garden Lane a prison van ('Black Maria'), which conveyed prisoners to and from the courts and to the city goal. In February 1907 it was decided to close down West Walls fire station and transfer the appliances to the central fire station and Junction Street.

In 1907 Council proceedings give us a comprehensive account of the Brigades Plant, dispersed throughout the city: 1 steam engine, a manual engine, a hose cart, tools, jumping sheets, and appliances at Spring Garden Lane; 1 fire escape with stand pipe, a hose, a hose cart and scaling ladders at West Walls, the system of the alarm bell was operated by an office clerk; 1 manual engine, a hose and a cart and appliances at Junction Street. 'There are twelve hand pumps at different parts of the city, 4430 feet of canvas hose and leather hose' (Sergeant Wakeford).

Part of the Police fireman's job was to give advice and instruction to various local institutions such as the Cathedral, or schools and hospitals in the usage of fire appliances. Similarly inspection of shops and warehouses, where gunpowder, petrol and other explosives were stored, was a statutory obligation. By 1909 the city Police had undertaken ambulance duties, the vehicle being pulled by horse. This service raised a revenue of £33.17s.9d in its first year of use; being paid for by the removal of private patients.

During this period the number of fires averaged 35. Exclusive of this statistic, in November 1911 Canonbie telegraphed the Police Office requesting assistance at a fire, but because the town did not pay a retaining fee aid was refused. An act which is comparable to the Bohemian Insurance Company fire brigades a hundred years earlier. If this mannerism could be compared, the equipment certainly could not. All appliances were kept in a condition of high efficiency, the boiler in fact being annually inspected by the independent Vulcan Boiler Insurance Company. In 1914 the brigade moved truly into the twentieth century, the manual fire engine was withdrawn from use and the steam engine used as cover in the event of fires until 'other arrangements were made'. Thus in Januari 1914 the Town Clerk applied to the Local Government Board for sanction to borrow £1,026 for the purchase of a motor fire engine – payable over a ten year period. In conjunction twenty uniforms and two bicycles were purchased and the two horses sold.

The new petrol-driven fire engine (HH 79), with first-aid outfit and 50 foot escape was delivered by Messrs. Merryweather & Sons early in September and subsequently driven by Sergeant Dugdale (later Inspector Dugdale). During its first year the engine turned out on thirteen occasions, the first-aid outfit being used where large quantities of water was not required.

The brigade at this stage in its development now renders some appearance to the efficient service we, today, perhaps take for granted. The members were trained professionals, the equipment mechanised, and their government sponsored resources growing at an ever increasing rate. These factors were imperative in an expanding city, as such was Carlisle.

The 1904 Watch Committee Report on the reorganisation of the City Brigade

To the Members of the Watch Committee of the City of Carlisle.

Gentlemen,

We, the deputation appointed by the City council to visit various towns in England in connection with the re-organisation of the Fire Brigade, beg to make the following recommendations as the result of a very exhaustive and careful study of the Fire Brigade systems in the various towns we visited, and from information obtained from many other places of which we had reports.

We visited Manchester, Lancaster, Wigan, St. Helens, Bootle, Southport, and Blackpool. Wherever we went we were particularly impressed with the fact that Carlisle, as compared with other towns of a similar and even smaller size, is very far behind in Fire Brigade organisation.

Many of the towns we visited, not much larger than Carlisle, had Fire Stations built and equipped at a cost in some cases from £20,000 to £30,000 and with large staffs of permanent firemen at an annual cost of upkeep of about £1,500 to £2,000.

We do not, of course, propose to emulate those towns in such an expenditure, but what we do recommend is the most modest scheme that can possibly be put before you, having due regard for economy and at the same time a sense of our responsibility to provide for the safety and well-being of the City. We are firmly of opinion from all the information we obtained from the various Chief Constables and Fire Masters that the Brigade of this City must be solely a Police Brigade, with the Chief Constable in charge of it.

We might take the opportunity at this junction of expressing to the Lord Mayor of Manchester, Mayors, Chairmen and Chief Constables of the towns we visited, our hearty appreciation of their kindness and willingness to provide us with all information and assistance in their power.

While recommending that the Police have sole charge of the Fire Brigade, we think it is only due to the Volunteer Fire Brigade that we should mark our approbation at this time of the good work they have rendered to the City in years gone by, and trust that they will show their goodwill to the Police Brigade in the future.

(1) We recommend that the Fire Brigade be a Police Brigade, and that the Police force be augmented by two thoroughly-trained firemen who understand the work connected with a fire brigade in all its branches, and that they be selected from a large Police Fire Brigade, where outbreaks of fire are of daily occurrence, one to be appointed with the rank of Sergeant with pay commencing at 34/- per week, rising to 40/-, and the other with the rank of first class Constable at 29/- per week, rising to 33/-, with free quarters, coal and light at Spring Gardens Lane, and that they devote their whole time and attention to fire brigade work, the keeping and repairing of all fire engines, hose pipes, and whole apparatus.

(2) That they drill and instruct the auxiliary Constable firemen in fire brigade work and carry out all duties, and observe all rules and regulations that are, or may be made, connected therewith, according to the instructions of the Watch Committee or the Director of the Fire Brigade.

(3) That 20 members of the force who have volunteered their services, be appointed firemen and receive 2s per week increase in pay, so long as they continue to act as firemen, this remuneration will cover all the work they are called upon to perform as firemen in the City, and attendance at drills, turnouts etc.

(4) That the buzzer be discontinued and each fireman's house be connected with the headquarters station by telephone at an estimated annual cost of £1.15s.0d per house for the purposes of the fire brigade and general matters connected with the Police force.

(5) That a telephone instrument be fixed in the gentlemen's public urinal in English Street and connected with the Police Office for the use of the Police and the public in cases of outbreaks of fire or other emergencies, and that the Constables in that district on night duty be supplied with keys giving them access thereto.

(6) That the Sub(Fire Brigade and Works)Committee, with the Chief Constable, confer with the Health Committee as to the purchase of two suitable horses for the fire brigade work, to be kept permanently at the Spring Gardens Fire Station, and also to make arrangements for a change of horses from the Corporation Yard.

(7) That a Constable fireman occupies the Junction Street Station, and provide accommodation for one or two single Constable firemen, and keep in good order the fire apparatus, etc., and that the house be also used as a sub-station for reporting and attending to any urgent Police business that may require to be communicated to the Central Office by telephone.

(8) That loose boxes be fitted up for the two horses at Spring Gardens fire station, and fire brigade harness obtained for the horses.

(9) That uniforms be obtained for the firemen, and that two chemical hand-engines be purchased at a cost of £4 each, and that a smoke helmet for firemen be purchased at a cost of about £20.

The foregoing recommendations can be carried out at an initial cost of £100 exclusive of horses, and that the firemen's wages and up-keep of horses etc., would amount annually to £270 or thereabouts.

In conclusion we need hardly add that these recommendations are made entirely with a view to securing a thoroughly efficient and economical fire brigade system for our City.

We have the honour to be
Gentlemen,
Your obedient Servants,
Signed,
DAVID LAING, Chairman
WM. PHILLIPS, Deputy-Chairman
GEORGE HILL, Chief Constable

Resolved — That the recommendations be submitted to the Council for adoption.

Police account of a major outbreak of fire
December 28th 1914

At 3.10 p.m. I received uniform 44 on from P.C. Walker by telephone from Police Office that fire had broken out at Morton's Mill and saying it was going. The Motor was immediately turned out and arrived quickly on the scene with 4 men on board. I found the fire had a good hold of the two top storeys of the 5 storey building. The hydrants were got to work at once, some of the firm's employees being already at work with the Company's hydrants in the yard. Owing to 2 carts which were leading flue dust blocking the passage to the drain a slight delay was caused before the Motor could be got to the drain and when got to work it could not be kept going for any length of time owing to the large crowd of unauthorised people who although willing to do whatever they could would not desist pulling, tugging and kinking the hose, thus throttling the engine to overpressure and causing it to stop. The same occurred in the case of the hydrants, 4 of which were broken and 3 being damaged so that they were rendered useless. As soon as I was able to stop this both the Motor and Steamers worked splendidly. The fire burned quickly and soon the whole roof came down with a crash — the two top floors followed immediately afterwards. We then concentrated our efforts to saving the Weaving Shed, Engine House and other adjoining buildings which we were fortunate enough to save, considering the fire had spread so rapidly.

The Motor Steamer was kept at work until the following day at noon when the Motor was returned to the station immediately after we had occasion to return the steamer again. While doing so Mr. inquired where the motor had gone and on being told said it was to be brought back and worked in place of the Steamer on account of the sparks it threw out, being afraid some would ignite the buildings in close proximity. The Motor was brought back and the Engine dispensed with. The Steamer returned to the station about 11 a.m. the Motor returning about 8 p.m. Several outbreaks broke out afterwards but were dealt with by hydrants.

Every effort was utilised to save any part of the building and I wish to give credit to the excellent work of the Firemen who I am sure worked most creditably.

The following private brigades attended and rendered valuable assistance, Carr & Co., Holme Head, Teasdale & Co. and the Castle.

I am pleased to have to report that no fatal accidents occurred. Two soldiers who were assisting were badly cut on the hand, several narrow escapes were also experienced by falling walls, timber etc.

Whilst visiting again at 10 a.m. on January 1st with the intention of removing more a huge portion of the wall on the weaving shed side of the Mill came down with a crash, fortunately no one being hurt, immediately after some salvage stock which had been thrown out of the building into the street caught alight which I extinguished and another two small outbreaks in other parts of the buildings, — returning to the station at 1 p.m.

At 5.30 p.m. on the same date I was sent for it having broken out again at the rear of the premises adjoining the Engine House and warehouse. I immediately proceeded there having left a standpipe etc for emergencies and got it to work.

Owing to the dangerous state of a gable end a Constable has been kept on duty to prevent persons congregating nearby, from 11 a.m. January 1st until 10 a.m. January 4th 1915.

Firemen present Chief Constable Sergeant Dugdale. Engineer Warwick and Hughes.
2.3.6.8.10.11.12.16.22.27.28.31.34.35.36.37.42.45. Bainbridge.

Damage about £50,000
Insured by Royal Insurance Co.
Fire Asst.. Insurance Co.
Caused by Spontaneous Combustion.

History and development of the City of Carlisle Fire Service 1866-1966

Although the history of Carlisle records that the City was virtually destroyed by fire on three occasions, i.e., in 1251, again in 1292 and finally in 1390; there is no record of any fire fighting parties until about the year 1800, when insurance companies began to take an interest in the protection from fire of those premises which were insured by them.

The first indication of any official fire fighting equipment in the City was published in Jollie's Guide of 1811. It is stated in the Guide: 'We think it necessary to mention that two engines are kept behind the East Walls. Unfortunately there are no firemen attached to them.'

In 1827 mention is made of a group of volunteer fire fighters when the Major issued an order that 'in case of fire, the practice of ringing the Town Hall bell should cease, as all it succeeded in doing was gathering improper persons at the scene, and brawling was not uncommon'. The year 1836 saw the advent of a volunteer fire brigade under the command of the Superintendent night watchman, but this project soon followed in the steps of any previous attempts to form a stabilised Fire Brigade. It was at this time that the first fire station was erected by public subscription in West Walls. Two manual fire engines were obtained with financial assistance of £100 grant from the City Council. These engines were called the 'Alert' and the 'City'. With the backing of the City's business men, Captain J.A. Wheatley reformed the Volunteer Brigade in 1866. It consisted of 32 officers and men with two manual pumps and subsidiary equipment. This brigade was called out to fires by the ringing of the Cathedral bells, and in one year attended the record number of four fires.

A new horse-drawn manual fire engine was developed in 1865 by Shand Mason & Co. One was purchased for Carlisle in 1870 and was stationed in the Junction Street Fire Station, which had just been completed. This machine remained in use until the arrival of the horse-drawn 'Steamer' in 1904. At this period the Fire Brigade was commanded by Captain J.J. Bell and during his term of office a new Fire Engine Station was opened in Spring Gardens Lane in 1902. This station was to remain the City's Fire Brigade Headquarters for the next 38 years.

Upon Captain Bell's retirement from service, Captain J. Little assumed command of the Brigade. His term of office continued until 1909, when Carlisle like so many other cities in the country, placed the control of the fire brigades in the hands of their Police force, with the appointment of Chief Constables as 'Directors of the Fire Brigade'. It was at this juncture, too, that ambulance duties were introduced to the City's Fire Brigade and a horse-drawn ambulance (Black Maria) was incorporated in the equipment.

The establishment of the brigade from then onwards consisted of policemen who carried out the dual duties of policing and fire fighting for which they received an extra 5s. per week. A permanent wholetime station sergeant was appointed, to whom the Chief Constable delegated the duties of Station Officer and Training Officer. In 1914 the first petrol-driven fire engine was purchased by the City Council. Later a second one was acquired and about 1918 a petrol-driven ambulance was purchased. These machines continued to do service until about 1932, when a new motor pump was purchased. In 1938 a limousine type of pump escape was bought.

This system of Police Fire Brigade continued until 1941 and the succeeding Chief Constables and Station Officers during these 32 years were as follows; the Chief Constables Hill, Spence, Johnston, Wilson and Lakeman, and Station Sergeants Wood, Dugdale, Gate and Todd, the latter three later in their careers being appointed as Inspectors. In 1940, during Chief Constable Lakeman's term of office, the Police and Fire Service moved into the present premises at Warwick Street. The estimated cost of the service was then approximately £2,300 per annum or the equivalent of a 1d. rate, with an establishment of ten wholetime personnel.

It was also in 1940 that the Government of the day realised that the resources of the country's fire brigades were strained to capacity by the continued raids and fire storms caused by Hitlers air force and it was obvious that a change was imminent to assist in pooling forces to combat the war time fires. On 18th August 1941, the National Fire Service was born and the fire brigades of the country became as one with liabilities for duty in any part of the United Kingdom. Women were also introduced into the service at this time, their duties being telephonists and control room attendants. The first Fire Service College was inaugurated and training on modern lines became a major part of the service. This was a big stride in the history of the Fire Service. The National Fire Service was disbanded in 1948 and fire brigades were returned to their respective local authorities with recommendations for establishment according to the classification of fire risk and population of the authority, the Brigade to be entirely separate from the Police.

Carlisle now appointed its first wholetime Chief Fire Officer, Mr. R. Todd, Grad. I. Fire E., who commanded the Brigade until his death in June 1957. The authorised establishment of the Brigade was made up to one Chief Officer, a Deputy Chief Officer, four Station Officers, 56 other ranks and three firewomen. The equipment consisted of two pump escapes, one pump, one turntable ladder (100ft.), and one water tender. Fire protection was to cover the City (area 6,092 acres) and by agreement with the Cumberland County Council 167 square miles of the surrounding county.

These arrangements continue at the present date.

In 1951, the City's Ambulance Service was again incorporated with the Fire Service and the Fire Brigade now became known as the City of Carlisle Fire and Ambulance Service. The number of ambulances was to be increased because of the introduction of the National Health Scheme and the total now became nine vehicles manned by 24 civilian ambulance driver/attendants.

The various estimates of cost of maintenance of the Service for 1965/66 are as follows: Fire Service rate borne: £71,563. This is equivalent to 6.82 pence in the £. Ambulance Service rate borne: £29,951. This is equivalent to 2.80 pence in the £. During 1965 the Fire Service attended to 1,015 calls and the Ambulance Service to 26,096 calls, with a total mileage of 119,508, conveying 48,115 patients.

The Service is also responsible upon request and by agreement to undertake periodical inspection of all fire appliances and equipment in commercial and industrial premises under the Shops, Offices and Railway Premises Act, 1963. Full powers of inspection are also carried out under the Petroleum Regulations 1928 Act and for Means of Escape, under Section 34 of the Factories Act. Apart from fire-fighting the Fire Service also undertakes special services of an emergency character for which their appliances may be suitable.

The service incorporates seven part-time retained firemen who are called out by siren to assist at large fires and in addition there are 34 auxiliary firemen (volunteers) who train with five self-propelled engines, a pipe-carrying unit, a hose layer, a radio Land Rover and two motor cycles for despatch work, all stationed at Auxiliary Fire Station at Kingstown.

Carlisle Volunteer Fire Brigade

Balance sheet to 8th August 1867

Dr.	£	s	d	Cr.	£	s	d
To Subscriptions	206	19	6	By Advertisements	28	6	6
" Enrolment Fees	8	12	6	" Boots	38	11	0
" Interest at Bank	0	11	3	" Tunics	63	14	6
				" Helmets	21	7	4
				" Belts & Hatchets	17	7	4
				" Wrenches	2	1	0
				" Lamps	1	5	0
				" Ropes & Hooks	0	17	3
				" Gymnasium	3	4	0
				" Stationary & Printing	12	16	7
				" Sundries	3	11	7
				" Cheque Book	0	2	1
				" Balance at Bank	22	18	11
	£216	3	3		£216	3	3

Stock Account: 1 Tunic; 4 Helmets; 1 pair of Boots; 5 Belts; 5 Hatchets and 5 Hose Wrenches.

We, the appointed Auditor, having examined the Brigade Accounts, hereby certify to their being found correct, and further beg to testify to the very able manner in which the duties pertaining to the Secretaryship have been performed.
Signed, JAMES LEES, ROBERT WESTRAY, JOHN HALLAWAY.

List of subscriptions

	£	s	d
Dean and Chapter	10	0	0
Sun Insurance Office, per Joseph Bendle	5	5	0
Phoenix Fire Insurance Office, per Isaac Cartmell	5	5	0
County Insurance Office, per J.A. Wheatley	5	0	0
Norwich Union Fire Insurance Co., per David Latimer	5	0	0
Royal Exchange Insurance Co., per Hubert Rawons	5	0	0
Manchester Insurance Co., per C. Thurnam & Son	5	0	0
Liverpool, London and Globe Insurance Co., per J. Sawyer	5	0	0
Royal Insurance Co., per W. Slater	5	0	0
Imperial Insurance Co., per H.J. Halton	5	0	0
Cumberland Union Banking Co.,	5	0	0
His Grace the Duke of Devonshire	5	0	0
The Lord Bishop of Carlisle	5	0	0
The Right Hon. the Earl of Lonsdale	5	0	0
Peter Dixon & Sons, Manufacturers	5	0	0
Carr & Co., Castle Street	5	0	0
Citadel Railway Station Committee	5	0	0
Henry Lonsdale M.D.	5	0	0
W. Marshall, Esq., M.P., Patterdale Hall	3	3	0
W.N. Hodgson, Esq., M.P.	3	3	0
Thomas Barnes, M.D.	3	3	0
E. Potter, Esq., M.P.	3	3	0
R. Ferguson, Morton	3	0	0
Cowans, Sheldon, & Co., St. Nicholas & Co., Manufacturers	3	0	0
G. Ferguson, Draper, Scotch Street	3	0	0
Messrs. Cust, Abbey Street	3	0	0
Lowthian & Fairlie, Manufacturers	2	2	0
S.J. Binning, Warwick Road	2	2	0
J.A. Wheatley, Jeweller	2	2	0
Very Rev. the Dean of Carlisle	2	2	0
C. & J. Armstrong, Builders	2	2	0
Mounsey & Son., Castle Street	2	2	0
R. & J. Steel, Carlisle Journal	2	2	0
Stead & McAlpin, Cummersdale	2	2	0
Atlas Fire Office, per J.C. Wannop	2	2	0
S. Blaylock, Abbey Street	2	2	0
North British and Mercantile Insurance Co., per S. Saul	2	2	0
Scottish Union Insurance Co., per J. Donald	2	2	0
Old Brewery Co.	2	2	0
J. Nanson, Town Clerk	1	10	0
T. Sewell, Saddler	1	7	6
A. Davidson, Devonshire Street	1	1	0
Rev. T.C. Durham	1	1	0
J. Hind & Co., Botchergate	1	1	0
T. Tweddle, Hatter	1	1	0
J. Graham, Timber Merchant	1	1	0
J. Routledge, Tobacconist	1	1	0
R. Buck, Dalston	1	1	0
J. Dacre, Kirklinton	1	1	0
Halstead & Pearson, English Street	1	1	0

	£	s	d
J. Mounsey & Co.	1	1	0
T. Hutton, Warwick Road	1	1	0
T.L. Bonnell, Lowther Street	1	1	0
Atkinson & Wood, English Street	1	1	0
Misses Wilson, Stanwix Bank	1	1	0
R. Armstrong, Draper, English Street	1	1	0
B. Scott, Devonshire Street	1	1	0
Carlisle City & District Bank	1	1	0
S. Saul & Son	1	1	0
J. Richardson, Dalston	1	1	0
A. Thompson, Chemist	1	1	0

Report of the Fire Engine Committee

That they have divided the five pounds given by the York and London Insurance Company and Mr. Brockbank as below. The Committee would further recommend that the thanks of the Committee be given to the Insurance Company for their liberal donation.

Police Officers

Mr. Graham Supt	5. 0
J. Glaister Night	3. 6
John Short	3. 0
Jos. Haigh	3. 0
Thos. Hetherington	3. 0
R. Robinson	2. 0
J. Johnston	2. 0

Mr. Porter's Foundry Men

F. Ruddick	2. 0	H. Dyer	3. 6
T. Court	2. 0	Davidson	2. 0
W. Storrow	2. 0	Atkinson	2. 0
R. K'patrick	2. 0	W. Farish	2. 0
I. Teasdale	2. 0	Rae	2. 0
T. Jordan	2. 0	Hodgson	2. 0
R. Graham	3. 0	Farish	2. 0
W. Graham	2. 0	M. Corcoran	3. 0	Webster	2. 0
D. Errington	2. 0	T. Mason	2. 0	Roberts	2. 0
R. Barnfather	2. 0	M. Monghan	2. 0	Burgess	2. 0
J. Howe	2. 0		2. 11. 6	Proudfoot	2. 0
Carried forward	1. 9. 6		18. 0		

City of Carlisle

List of Charges for the attendances of the Fire Brigade at fires without the City.

Foreman: for the first hour or portion theron, if engine is worked — 3/-;
for each succeeding half hour or portion thereof — 1/-;
for turn out only — 3/6.

Engineer or Sergeant: for the first hour or portion thereof if engine is worked — 3/-;
for each succeeding half hour or portion thereof — 1/-;
for turn out only — 3/-.

Firemen: each for first hour or portion thereof if engine is worked — 2/6;
each for every succeeding half hour or portion thereof — 9d;
each for every hour or portion thereof watching after fires — 9d;
each for turn out only — 2/6.

Assistants: 1/- per man for first hour, and 6d for each succeeding hour.

Engines and Appliances (if worked): each per hour or portion

thereof up to the first 3 hours £1.1;
each per hour or portion thereof after the first 3 hours 10/6.
Engines and Appliances (not worked):
each for turn out only 21/-.
Appliances: per day or portion thereof for appliances left after fires to cool debris 21/-.
Horse hire: horse hire will be charged according to time and number of horses engaged.
Damages to engines and implements not being the result of ordinary wear and tear will be charged in addition to the foregoings.

Extract from Cumbria Fire Service Annual Report 1992-1993

CUMBRIA FIRE SERVICE

- is one of the major Emergency Services in Cumbria, providing immediate assistance to the public in a wide range of emergency situations:
- has over 700 full and part-time personnel providing a continuous firefighting capability from 38 fire stations countywide;
- is responsible to the Public Protection Committee of the Cumbria County Council, who are the statutory Fire Authority;
- maintains a comprehensive countywide communications system providing a speedy response to emergency calls received;
- has a statutory duty to attend all fire calls within prescribed times;
- attends a wide range of non-fire emergency calls where life and/or property are threatened;
- promotes fire safety throughout the County, actively persuing a reduction in the number of fires occurring;
- provides a safety training service to business and industry in the County;
- provides a fire estinguisher sales and maintenance service;
- represents Cumbria's interests in regional, national and European forums involved with fire safety and firefighting provisions;
- persues the protection of the environment by pollution control activities, and the use of environmentally friendly materials wherever possible;
- pursues a policy of equal opportunities in respect of appointments and promotions;
- seeks to ensure the Health and Safety of all personnel employed.

Chief Fire Officer J.M. Elliott Esq., Cert. Mi Fire E

Cumbria Fire Service Headquarters

Modern Control Room. The total number of staff: 286 wholetime, 433 retained, 18 control, 51 non uniform, total 788.

This is the Cumbria badge as it is to-day.

Carlisle Fire Station, Warwick Street 1995, Now 'C' Division Cumbria County Fire Service: the Red Watch, Blue Watch, White Watch and Green Watch.

1   The author of this book as a young fireman: James Parker Templeton.

2   The Carlisle Volunteer Fire Brigade with the horse-drawn manual pump. Note the outriders, or postillions in uniform. Their job was to handle the horses.

3   Captain J.A. Wheatley and the C.V.F.B. on an outing to Low Gelt near Brampton circa 1875.

4 Captain J.A. Wheatley, the first Chief of Carlisle V.F.B. As you will see on the photograph he was also Mayor of Carlisle.

5 Captain John Bell, 2nd Chief of C.V.F.B.

6 Captain James Little, the 3rd Chief of C.V.F.B.

7   Robert Todd, 4th Chief Fire Officer, the brigade now no longer under the Police, and now Carlisle City Fire Service – 1940.

8   Francis 'Frank' Lorrigan, M.B.E., Q.F.S.M., 5th Chief Fire Officer. Frank became chief following the death of Chief Fire Officer R. Todd.

9   Captain J.A. Wheatley and Lt. J. Bell with a group of the C.V.F.B. circa 1875.

10   Captain J. Bell on the left of the photograph standing, also wearing his silver helmet.

11   Captain J. Bell's silver helmet, now in Carlisle Tullie House Museum.

12   Capt. John Bell and Lt. James Little with the C.V.F.B.

13   This photograph of the Volunteers was taken during a Whit Monday holiday outing, to give the men an airing, and the horses exercise. If a fire broke out in the meantime, a messenger was promptly despatched on a bike to inform the brigade.

14   Here we have the horses at Spring Gardens Lane Fire Station; the driver was Tom Warwick and the horses were named David and George. The former was named after David Ling, Chairman of the Fire Brigade, and George after George Hill, Chief Constable.

15   Captain James Little: the volunteers and the steam fire engine. The 'Steamer' was purchased in 1904.

16   Captain J. Little standing on the right of the large wheel with some of the members of his brigade. Note the hand cart on the left, which was used for carrying articles of equipment, but used mainly for carrying any-one injured, so it was really an early ambulance.

17   This is the new steam fire engine on a trial outing seen near the Old Turf Hotel. The man wearing the light suit is Mr. George Hill, Chief Constable. The man on the right, wearing bike clips, is Bob Gate.

18   During the long history of the Fire Brigade the city has had five main fire stations. The Shambles off Scotch Street was the first. This old entrance is still visible.

19   This was the second station situated on West Walls (now demolished).

20   This photograph shows the panelled door at the entrance to Junction Street Fire Station (now demolished). This was the third station and had a house attached for the officer in charge.

21 Spring Gardens Lane was the fourth station. Opened in 1898 and used until the beginning of the war.

22 Warwick Street Fire Station opened in 1940. It was one of the most up-to-date in England, with automatic doors etc. and is still in use today as C Division Cumbria Fire Service (Station No. 5).

23   The Merryweather HH79 and engine number two. Next we had the first petrol-driven ambulance to come into use in the city, and finally the Black Maria or police van, all at Spring Gardens Lane. The driver of HH79 is Tom Warwick and the driver of engine No. 2 is Bob Gate, the officer in charge standing between.

24   Robert Todd, who later became Carlisle Chief Fire Officer, as a young man (standing). He began work in Carlisle in 1928 as an A.A. man.

25   Firemen outside Morton Park House. Left to right: Robert Todd, Norman Jackson, Bob Gate, Davidson and Billy Robinson. Note the navy-type hats with a bow of ribbon; at this time these men were classed as Police Firemen.

26   Carlisle City fire engine. Driving is Sergeant R. Todd, seated in the centre is B. Rae and at the rear is fireman John Scott. The Cub was purchased in 1938 and classed as a limousine type pump escape.

27   The new limousine pump escape at Warwick Hall fire circa 1938. The Hall was severely damaged but later rebuilt.

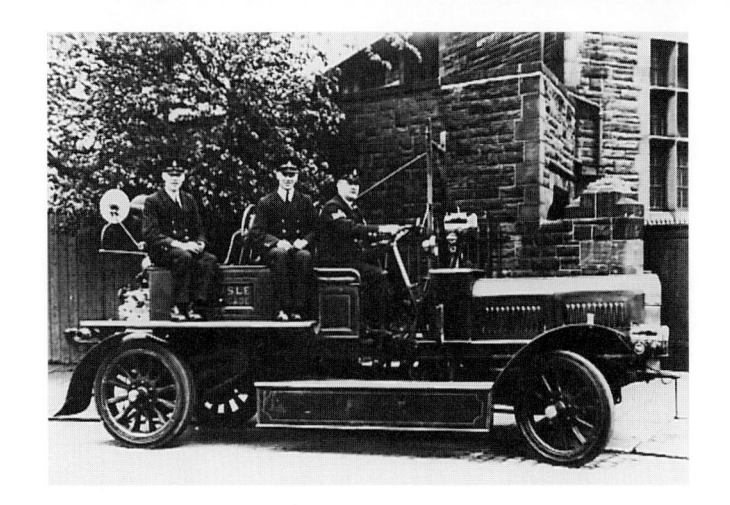

28 Her Majesty's Theatre, Carlisle, destroyed by fire on 15th September 1904, from a painting by Phetan Gibb. The show at the theatre at that time was 'The Country Girl'.

29   Old appliances outside Warwick Street Fire Station having been on show to the public, and the modern 100 ft T.L. in the background.

30   Note the long centre shaft on the old steamer for coupling the horses, and next to that the 10 man manual pump (hard work).

31   These fire insurance signs were attached to buildings insured by whichever company. If you had paid your insurance, that company would help to put out your fire with their brigade, if not you could burn. Only one fire insurance sign remains on a building in Carlisle! The signs on this photograph are now in Carlisle's Museum.

32 Police volunteers and Watch Committee outside the Grammar School with the steam engine, note the police helmets.

33 Fireman A. Steele showing off a fine example of a police brass fire helmet and beard to match!

34 Police firemen outside Spring Gardens Lane with the Merryweather. Tom Warwick, the engineer, is wearing a police brass helmet.

35   The pump escape with its 60 ft ladder. The engine was a 65 H.P. Leyland Tiger. The two crew members are fireman L. Cowan and fireman R. Birkett. (Registration No. BHH 1.)

36   A view from the T.L. showing the men ready to house the escape ladder onto the pump escape.

37   This vehicle was converted on the station and used for towing a light pump. (Circa 1952.)

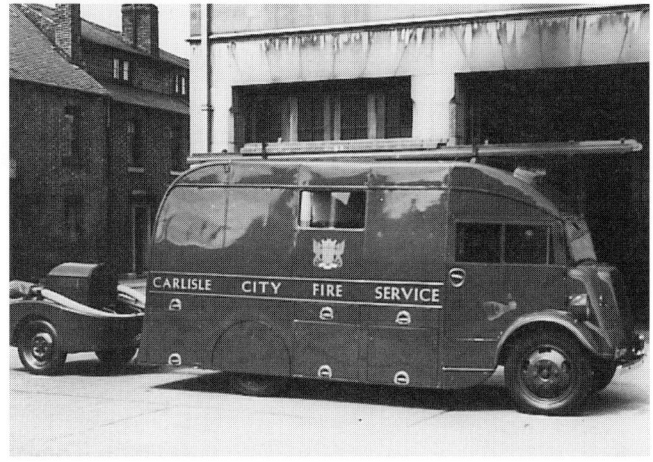

38   This vehicle was known as a wartime A.T.V. and capable of towing pumps, heavy or light, as used during the blitz in wartime Britain. Many fire brigades used them long after the war. Here are firemen Bill Irving and L. Cowan.

39   The modern pump escape (P.E.), powered by a Rolls Royce engine, again carrying the up-to-date 60 ft escape hose reels, search lights and all the equipment to deal with a large outbreak of fire, circa 1960.

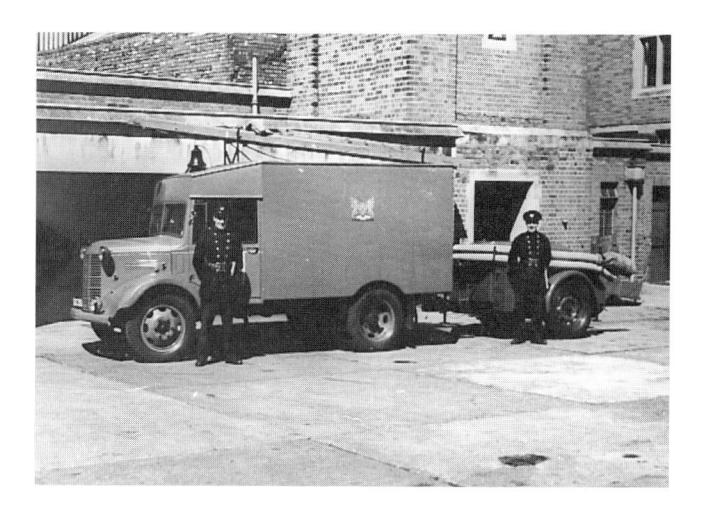

40   GHH 827 known as the S.P. (special pump) again powered by a Rolls Royce engine. No escape ladder as such, but carrying a 30 ft ladder and short ladders. This engine usually attended most fires, City or rural.

41   The 100 ft turntable ladder made by Merryweather, photographed in the fire station yard circa 1953.

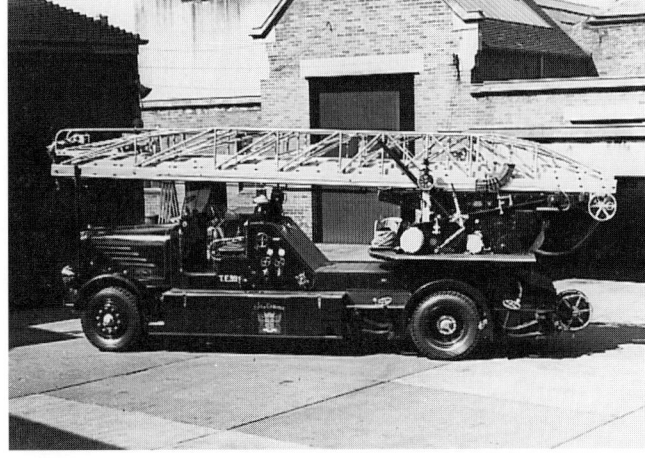

42 Sub Officer John Scott with the fire prevention van. John would now be termed as the fire safety officer (not fire prevention).

43   Ropes are a very important piece of equipment as far as a fireman is concerned, and before use were always tested by the weight of six men, as seen here.

44   Guide lines being tested by two men. These lines were used to steady the escape during high winds.

45   Sub Officer Sid Phillips, head mechanic and in charge of all vehicle repairs, keeps an eye on work being done on the Leyland Tiger. The other fireman mechanic is Joe Underwood.

46   A daily routine job was to keep everything spotless. Here fireman Jim Bullen and fireman R. Birkett are polishing all the brass fittings on the T.L.

47   Still on routine cleaning polishing floors. Note the brass pole and drop to the floor below. This was the fast way down to the fire engine.

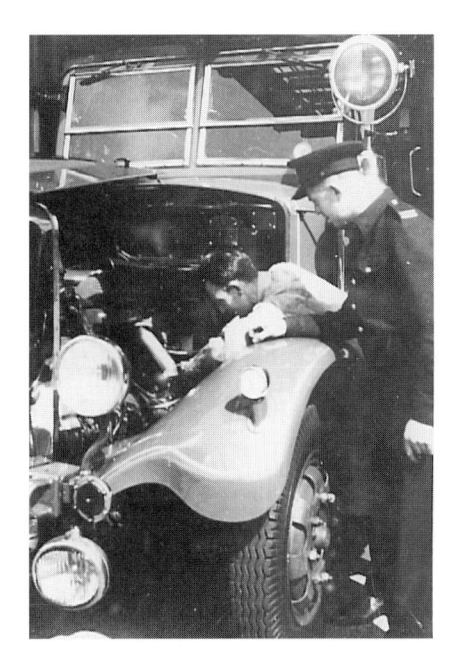

48   Station Officer A. Bird and crew after a severe fire in the Botchergate area. Further fireman J. Sewell, fireman Dick Graham, Sub Officer H. Hale and fireman Jack McKinlay.

49   This photograph shows the hose store where all the hose not in use is checked daily and stored ready for use if required. You see here Sub Officer E. Gardner checking the brass couplings and fireman R. Foster checking the hose numbers.

50   Some firemen up aloft, being watched by the fire crew on regular drills. Sub Officer Bert Irons is in charge.

51   Hook ladders being used to climb from one floor to the next and so on. Now they are no longer in use.

52   Three men have scaled the tower (or building) have hooked on to the fixed ring on the ladder and lean back with arms extended, showing full confidence in their equipment. Not for the faint-hearted!

53   Fireman returning from hook ladder drill, accompanied by Sub Officer Hale in charge.

54   Fireman's lift carrying down the 60 ft escape from the second floor window. This was also a routine drill.

55   Foam drill in the fire station yard, also to test the quality of the foam, that may have to be used on large oil or petrol fires.

56   Hoses and pumps in use during an annual inspection being carried out by H.M.'s Inspector of Fire Brigades.

57   The annual inspection of Carlisle City Firemen by Her Majesty's Inspector of Fire Brigades, the Mayor, Mr. Routledge and council officials.

58 Annual Inspection by H.M.'s Inspector of Fire Brigades, who is followed by the Mayor of Carlisle. Mr. Partridge is accompanied by Mr. Lancaster and Chief Fire Officer R. Todd.

59 Annual Inspection by H.M.'s Inspector, the Mayor, Miss Sibson and Chief Fire Officer F. Lorrigan.

60 The nerve centre of the Fire Station, the control room; in charge is leading firewoman S. Temple, assisted by Miss E. Dawson. The term firewoman has now been replaced with the word firefighter.

61   During a long, cold, wet and nasty job a cat was rescued from under Denton Street, Carlisle. It had somehow got into the millrace and perched on some wreckage under the street. Finally recued the cat ran off home!

62   This vehicle was used for carrying the large 6" plastic pipes used during the days of the Auxilliary Fire Service (AFS).

63   Here you see another use for the plastic pipes. Sub Officer Hale demonstrates how to prepare the pipes by blocking the ends, and making ready to cross the loch by the aid of a light pump.

64   Don your life jackets or prepare to swim, but all seems to be working out on Thurstonfield Loch.

65   Chief Fire Officer R. Todd, Deputy F. Lorrigan, Sub Officer John Donnelly and men of the AFS Carlisle.

66   These are emergency 'dams', used by the wartime Fire Service for storing water to supply fire engines in various parts of the town. Water was pumped from the nearest stream or river to fill these emergency dams. On many of the streets painted in yellow you can still see the letters EWS and an arrow pointing to the nearest open water.

67   Pumps at the river Eden supply water to the 'dams' mentioned in photograph No. 66 also supply water directly to the fire; similar to the fire seen on the next photograph.

68 Green Goddess fire engines used by the NFS and AFS and a group of Carlisle AFS firemen. Sub Officer Donnelly is in charge.

69 A full scale exercise on Eden Bridge with regular firemen and NFS firemen. Note the pipe carrier at the back of the three Green Goddess fire engines. Station Officer F. Lorrigan is in charge.

70 A large woodland and heath on fire.

71   One of the varied jobs a fireman might encounter: here Carlisle firemen are called to pump the Roman Well dry at the Castle to search for stolen goods. Leaning on the wall is Mr. E. Blezard from Carlisle Museum, also Station Officer F. Lorrigan and a fireman.

72 A more pleasant job: fireman L. Cowan directing school children and teacher round the Fire Station.

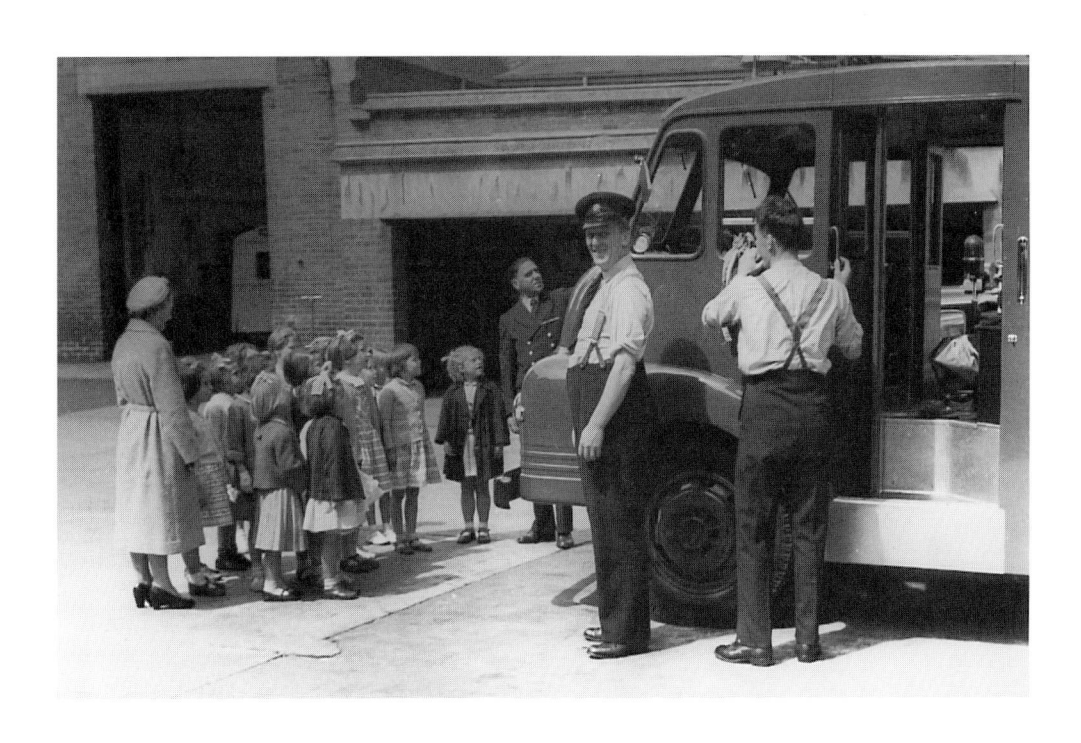

73   One way of getting water over the main road. Again using the plastic and metal pipes and no interruption or hold up to traffic.

74   Firemen on Sunday stand down.

75   Red Watch Carlisle City Fire Service.

76   Fire at Scott's Leather Works and going well because of the chemicals and fats.

77   The Newtown Co-operative store on fire. Note the 60 ft escape in use.

78   Tyre dump on fire. This blaze could be seen for miles because of the dense black smoke and it took a week before it was declared out. Station Officer E. Hall and fireman J. Wright.

79   Teasdale's sweet factory well alight. This was in the Denton Holme district of Carlisle and several homes had to be evacuated. (Circa 1973.)

80   West Walls Fire at the rear of the Carlisle Journal newspaper building. Well alight. Fireman W. Sharkey wearing breathing apparatus evacuating the building – in other words 'getting out quick'.

81/82   The firemens' children's Christmas party 1958 at Carlisle City Fire Station, Warwick Street.

83   Carlisle firemen on the Armistice Parade, circa 1953; most having served in the forces previous to joining the Fire Service.

84 Carlisle Fire Service taken by fireman Jim Templeton at Warwick Street. Chief Fire Officer R. Todd is seated in the centre. Front row firewoman E. Dawson and leading firewoman S. Temple on the left. On the right Josephine Richardson and Muriel Mitchell.